T0163907

THE SETS

THE SETS

Victor Billot

OTAGO UNIVERSITY PRESS
Te Whare Tā o Te Wānanga o Ōtākou

Published by Otago University Press
Te Whare Tā o Te Wānanga o Ōtakou
Level 1, 398 Cumberland Street
Dunedin, New Zealand
university.press@otago.ac.nz
www.otago.ac.nz/press

First published 2021
Copyright © Victor Billot
The moral rights of the author have been asserted.

ISBN 978-1-98-859260-2

A catalogue record for this book is available from the National Library of New Zealand. This book is copyright. Except for the purpose of fair review, no part may be stored or transmitted in any form or by any means, electronic or mechanical, including recording or storage in any information retrieval system, without permission in writing from the publishers.

No reproduction may be made, whether by photocopying or by any other means, unless a licence has been obtained from the publisher.

Editor: Emma Neale
Cover photograph by Victor Billot
Author photograph by Susie Ripley

Printed in New Zealand by Southern Colour Print

CONTENTS

PART FOUR

ENVOI

ACKNOWLEDGEMENTS

PROLOGUE

.

THE SETS

In the east the swell pulses. The sets come on.
There is nothing out there except pattern and salt,
a drowned continent snoozing out millennia.
The ocean is of a whole. Division is our game.
After the storm, silence and inspection. Unrecognition.
Slough and crush. Branches compiled in boneheaps.
The low sun brushes evening's skirt, a soft hum on my skin.
A sense of other futures flows through me.
I tread parallel to skittering foam, alone with a sea
I imagine as female, and find a thin contentment.
Malachite shallows encoded for latitudes
where light bleaches away the ache of life.
Simpler now to walk into the day, into unlived possibility.
I dream of loss as freedom. But blood speaks.
I am still (after everything) human,
because fine bones and a glance across a loud room
can say enough. This is so close, you could touch it.
There is not much time and soon enough comes rest.
I wish these demands would forsake me,
my heart and balls and guts tangled hopelessly
in the murky business of the world.
Distant raging darkness beyond the line of the horizon
makes the ocean tremble, and so the sets come on.

PART ONE

LOCATION, LOCATION

My youngest has annexed the parental bed,
his entrance announced by murmured complaint.
I surrender my place and adjourn to his room
where I listen to the stillness of milk-warm night.
Above the shadow, the clouds have pulled back
their curtains. The belt of Orion:
three pricks of white, identified by my smartphone.
Modern convenience. Mintaka is the dimmest of the trio,
claimed by Arab sky gazers lost in pre-app antiquity.
Twin star, two siblings locked in eternal dance,
a tremble of light 900 years old.
In darkness I calculate income and outgoings,
debts, obligations, peeling paint on weatherboards,
annual leave. The weight of time is announced
by a sour pressure on my bladder.
I piss forlornly, sleep-wrapped, weary.
The world is now run by my generation.
How do any of us know what we are doing?
This time, no reply from Google.
Distant cores of stars burn away, burn away
their light, their substance.

LIFE IN THE PERMIAN

There is an exhibition about Monsters of the Permian:
they roamed the planet before the dinosaurs.
They look the same to me, with big gnashers and claws.

I need cash. Don't we all? Lunchtime comes.
I walk with a heavy bag to the second-hand bookshop
which buys and sells. I sell only. My library is thinning.

The Permian, all 46.7 million years of it, was jammed
between the Carboniferous and Triassic periods,
and featured the supercontinent Pangaea. True fact.

I make small talk with Richard behind the counter.
Walk away with my $30, feeling halfway between
20 and 70 million years old in the Mortgagearian Epoch.

As well as reptiles, there were Permian creatures
that were kind of proto-mammals:
hairy little fuckers with mean eyes.

I paid for my children to see that exhibition.
They read wall panels about *the great dying.*
The gigadeaths of the great and small.

That's how the Permian concluded: *the great dying.*
That's what they call it. Lava floods.
Methane clathrates. Aridity. Acidity. Anoxia.

I search for the two bills in my wallet: a twenty and a ten.
Gone. Nothing there. I look again as if
they could magically reappear.

After *the great dying*, it took ten million years for life
to get back to something resembling normal.
(The hairy little fuckers hid under rocks.)

Now I'm standing in front of a sign
advertising the Permian Monsters,
as I rifle through my pockets, in rage, in anguish.

Then a bit later on it all got smashed again
by the killer asteroid 65 million years ago,
and the HLFs were the only game left in town.

I'm searching for my missing cash
as killer asteroids explode on my head
on this fucking planet, this planet of death.

A BOY

A boy has fallen into sleep.
His face indistinct in submarine light,
curtains pulled on summer night.
Drawing air through parted lips,
untidy arms flung across sheets.
At rest from the tasks of waking day,
to run and shout, to laugh, to play.
Crimson blood half mine, a thread unwinds
stitched from stirring life in limitless time.
His brother sleeps too, in another bed.
What lies ahead?
My heart is scratched by love's sharp claw
as I watch quietly from the shadowed door.

602

(The train is not the journey)
streets empty but soaked with cold light
darkness holds the avernal drone
the machine of chambers sails through the storm
sidereal night, old night
pouring like ink cloud from the south
the strangeness of separation
as time groans back
revealing impossible rivers
and spectres on every street
dislocated time, dislocated place
the boundary between each possibility
grows sliver thin
the life that has become yours
trailing its bloody strands
from creation to dissolution
so seldom stations of rest
(The train is not the journey)

THE VISITOR

Disaster came up the street.
I heard his voice
behind the ragged hedge.
I walked out, into the day.
We shared a moment
in the summer light.
He spoke of things I hardly remember
and gently told me, *it's not your fault, you know.*
These things happen all the time.
The house melted behind me.
The box collapsed in my arms
and everything spilled across the path.
We stood together, watching.
There was nothing else to say.

FACEBOOK SENDS A MEMORY

Facebook sends a memory
of the then preceding now:
child and mother sunk
under summer's glow.
Things were good
and things were bad.
Pixels map deceits
that hold sweet truth.
This tactless friend
exhumes dead time
from layered ash.
Now child has grown
into the future's gash.
As midnight creeps,
tap, swipe and pinch.

COLLECTION

'Each of us bears his own Hell'

[Virgil, *The Aeneid*, Book VI, line 743]

In the front yard the gate sticks; too late now to fix.
Bikes tumbled in uncut grass offer domesticity.
Wrong. The children scream in rage and fright.
Their world a burning boat. You wrap one in your arms.
His legs whirl and kick. He wants to come with you:
not the other. Not his brother, who wails uncomprehending.
Horror circles overhead. The street silent as church.
Insides flayed raw, the power of speech excised.
Their mother stares at you and any love there was once
is in that boat and burning too.

CAPUT MORTUUM

I know what I have done.
I know it had to be done.
An amputation.
Days arrive and disappear into the what has been.
After weeks, months, years of glue and blood,
keeping it breathing, I take the thing
and smash it completely, with resolute despair,
leaving scattered remains.
We stitched it all together from air
a long time ago, and now join the riven,
the vast common sob of the multitude.
I follow instruction manuals
for an age of unravelling, of disintegration,
of makeshift contingency.
An ache swells and fades,
buried in my bones and guts.
The shock of remembering
each time I look up from a screen
makes me dizzy, breathless with terror.
I have lost myself
and life falls away from under me
and my bundled possessions,
from the prepared explanation for children
who witness the rending and wailing,
and ask with polite concern *who will look after me?*
I know what I have done.
I know it had to be done.

AN OFFICE WORKER CONTEMPLATES THE PACIFIC OCEAN

Sea mist lifts by noon. *Thin sun glistens*
on the slick. The tide slips from
basalt slabs. *Coast stitched by*

wandering birds. Lunch a quick hour.
Removed from anxious hum of work world,
drained of love world. Walk on.

Old wharf broken mouth of timber.
Gate to a dark plutoid. Wrecked smile.
Lost time. Year past blank as sand.

Untranslatable. *Summer of final things.*
Relief of defeat. *Waves collapse gently.*
My being shivers. *Stroked by pills.*

To walk into the still day unmoored
from the past. *To be an absence.*
A failure of intent.

Children. Scheduled. *Formalised*
understanding. The state intercedes
to transfer funds for care.

Locked charts. Desire silenced.
A shiver of possibility.
Sleeping under deep snow.

LITANY

I gift these curses all to you,
a man whom I do not know and never will.
I curse your face, staring from the mirror.
I curse your hands, to twist in claws, arthritic.
I curse your heart and limbs: may they be strong,
to carry you for many barren years.
I curse your cock, so you piss crooked on the floor.
I curse your seed to worthless paste.
(This is mercy for the young you'll never know.)
I curse your laughter as it croaks dry in your gullet.
I curse your heart, so you never know the grace of love.
I curse your plans that come to pass, that they will never satisfy.
Like a worm that gnaws your guts, may you carry this litany inside.
I curse the waters, so they cannot slake your thirst.
I curse you when you lie groaning in death's jaws,
for you will not be ready, and you will dread the earth.
These words are just to fix your gaze on what must be seen.
So you have understanding, I curse all the years to come.
I curse you with knowledge, so you see what you have done.

ON THE RUN

Wet muzzle. Cold strings of drool.
The beast tracks me through streets.
I'm on the run.
My sister said, I thought it had missed you, and so did I.
I learned later on than some, who complete their fuck-ups young.
Not like these stumbling steps through trackless mud. No exit yet.
Shove the rubbish down within, black bags into rubbish bins.
It's the attrition does us in. There is no light, but gravity
binding us with groaning ropes, to children, loyalty, scarred hope,
fear of pain, the blank unknown. And what of love?
The bruise of silence lengthens. There are too many rooms
with doors rusted fast, where we are held by speechless rule.
Wet muzzle. Cold strings of drool.
The beast tracks me through streets.
I'm on the run.

STRAIGHT AND CLEAR

There was love, somewhere back there.
Somewhere back there, I knew at first sight,
on a road that once ran straight and clear.

Innocent of rancour, without bitter tears,
we danced and drank before dawn's clean light.
There was love, somewhere back there.

Love became a rusted claw to snare.
In unlife we snarl, tear and bite
on a road that once ran straight and clear.

Time has no remorse, no care,
as we scrape and bleed bone white.
There was love, somewhere back there.

Still I tremble for distant years,
for sometimes love was sometimes right
on a road that once ran straight and clear.

But burdened under weight we could not bear,
our way was lost in night
on a road that once ran straight and clear.
There was love, somewhere back there.

STRAY LIGHT

Today was the strangest day.
There are some hours left to drain from it.
There have been other days, strange enough.
I swore gutter-mouthed in cold corridors,
cursed warring children in the back seat,
was offered advice by people
whose names I did not know,
watched vivisections in passive horror
in the company of lawyers and shrinks.
In the crushed light of evening,
a golem wearing my trousers stalks
with demented fix on sulphuric horizons,
a cosmos programmed by hostile Galaxians.
In time the strange becomes the expected,
slumbering in wait to eat you from the inside out.
No strangeness in these wounds.
But today between roots of pain
growing through bereft earth, stray light filtered.
So strange and unfamiliar to sense a stirring of life,
and to fear it more than oblivion.

THE TERRAIN

Wake for night's interval at 3.30am.
Stand and sway dizzy, organise limbs.
Navigate the corridor in the dark,
on interior maps follow traces, marks
to a destination beyond sea, beyond day.
Stumbling without papers in the terminal,
metamorphic rooms, cities stranded
in past lives. Taxis speed through junctions
in a mute dawn. Clouds mass before the storm.
Sleek trains howl through oneiric streets.
Still, closer somehow, a woman is by my side.
Friend, muse, lover, lost self,
she is showing me the way.

IN THE WORLD

I take your hand that shapes the world.
I touch your arm by the thorn's crimson mark.
I lie in a dim room, the sea in your hair.
I kiss the soft moon of your breast.
I hold your hips that are meant to be held by me.
Radiance rushes through me when you smile.
I laugh in conspiracy with your sly grin.
I inhale your skin of bread, grass, mist.
When I am away from you I await all these things.
I am not familiar with this greed that fills me.
This requirement to hold, to possess, to be haunted.
In your silence and murmur, when we are together,
my heart recognises your heart.
In this recognition my heart cries out in gentle pain.

THE SHAPE OF THINGS

Driving the black ribbon around the bay,
fish-scale sea high on murmuring light,
memory caught me by surprise and flooded in.
For a moment I faltered: my head swum.
The past can do that. We inhabit time's mirage.
To forget is mercy. To remember, a cost.
Do we belong to the world, or does the world belong to us?

The dead's ventriloquy speaks from our lips.
Life's quantum flickers within our silent skulls.
Love cools. We corrode. We never really know anyone.
I can smell green wetness, hear midnight rain popping
on the tent's thin membrane. At the time,
they were all of life, those distant faces and voices.
Do we belong to the world, or does the world belong to us?

The days and dreams of southern towns can chill.
I pull curtains on sprawling darkness in the east.
Gather what I can. The past is past.
The shape of things grew malign and brittle.
I could not give my children what I had.
What I expected is not what I found.
We belong to the world, and this world belongs to us.

A SEA WIFE

Disorientation on the turn of soft winter,
walking is a controlled fall along the ocean's lip.
Liquid light drowning.
Memory rises from amniotic fathoms,
smudged shapes in the fog of war.
I inspect these artefacts from out of time.
Revenants gather on the edge of my vision.
I push them away and drown their murmur.
Numbed relief in the shimmer of white noise.
Fire and ice have burrowed deep.
Stunned by the commonplace,
the modern ways unhinge, derail my intent.
Salt drifts, humid, abrasive, quickening me.
The future is inveigling tide,
the *hiss-shhh* of glistening fronds
exhausted on patient sands.
I walk beside my sea wife.
How thin this life is to balance on.
How it shifts underneath me as I fall onwards
on an indeterminate ribbon of coast.

AN AZTEC JESUS RETURNED TO THE STREETS OF ATLANTIS

[With thanks to Andrew Spittle for the title]

Four men are silently waiting on damp tiles,
sitting at polite distances from one another.
Cardboard signs: HOMELESS AND HUNGRY. PLEASE HELP.
The first, a Māori in a hi viz jacket, says hello.
The last, further down the street, has no written statement.
He silently dictates his Pākehā vision of God,
locked within a home-made yoke,
head and arms clamped in medieval stocks.
In times past, a circle may have formed,
to jeer, pray, seek wisdom in these torments.
Lost within a mind run wild
amidst the mêlée of Sabbath shopping,
teenagers roll their eyes, 'Oh fuck',
the army of the median parting and surging
around his stricken features, gazes averted
as from a leper's deformations.
I promised my boys aniseed balls,
and they skipped past, accepting all as children do.
When later we talk about it,
the oldest says, *I felt kind of sorry for them.*
Then he repeats an overheard refrain:
It's a hard world out there.

GALLIMAUFRY

It could be diet, emotional state,
or pills red and white as festive party favours,
but I dream of toilets: toilets that won't flush,
doorless and exposed, overflowing like waterfalls.
I dream of running through the Underground
along shrunken, dwarvish tunnels,
boarding trains to unknown stations.
I dream of mysterious hills in another London,
of stairwells and rooms, wives, lovers, unfamiliar women,
rain, stolen cars, jet planes. I dream of lost cities,
of searching for an entrance to a nameless room.
I dream in panic the children are hurt, or vanished,
I dream of flats never lived in,
of visiting strangers in foreign apartment blocks.
I dream of exams I cannot find.
I dream of weeping, of rock bands, of barbers,
of the glaucous sea, of supermarket aisles,
of messages and chores and errands,
of terrible things on the edge of recollection.
I dream that my mind has been colonised
by electronic crackles from Radio Nowhere.
I dream I am a submarine beast.
I dream of life at seven,
and in these dreams the seen and unseen
flow through unguarded portals
and peel away in coils of smoke
through the rough hands of morning.

THE CRACK

There is a crack in the glass
of a window in my parents' house.
A jagged branch splits the light
and I look at it uneasily, wondering
if it might spread like a web, splintering,
but it never has, it's been there for years,
a fracture in their view of the grey Pacific.
They have learned to live with it, because
the cost of fixing some things is too great.
The crack remains, and no-one mentions it.
It has been accepted and we have moved on.
When my children come to stay,
I sleep on a mattress on the lounge floor.
The crack remains on the edge of my vision,
balanced between clarity and implosion.

VOICE IN DARKNESS

A voice speaks in darkness,
speaks, speaks,
to no one and to everyone,
from dreams of day to dreams of night,
from cluttered sheds of ninety years
now cut loose from memory's roots,
speaks whether there is no one here,
or someone in the listening chair
in this room of ending things,
of drawers of dry folded linen,
a wordless, useless, ink-dry pen.
Then with sudden lucid light,
a voice speaks of a long-dead wife,
mother of children, host to life,
a voice speaks and cracks
as if it happened yesterday.
A voice speaks in darkness,
speaks, speaks,
to no one and to everyone.

SNOW

David, Dick, I mean,
are you still working at the railways?
They look after me. It's a kind of hotel.
I'm not sure why they put me here.
Where are you now, up the Valley?
They're all darkies you know.
It's good enough I suppose.
She always comes out with a cup of tea.
Foreman said he felt crook,
went home for lunch.
They went round later
and he was on the bed, dead.
The finishing school—
that's where they put them, painting drums.
Parakeets. We used to catch them.
What's the good of it?
I used to ring up and you could make a bet.
Who's this bastard with a dog collar on his neck?
Camped in the river bed in the Bedford,
it was all right in summer.
The weasel ran between the spokes
and he fell off the bike.
She wouldn't go into hospital.
Publican said I'd been sampling the merchandise.
Told him where to.
Manpowered.
Veni vidi vici.

He got down the cane.

Look at them on the TV now.

Maggots on a dungheap.

Malaysia tin mines, just before the war.

From the old country.

Wanted $3 for a jug.

Jack said who farted? We all moved down the bar.

Jesus, he said, it's following us!

You can't get inside these new engines.

Cylinders, gaskets.

Took the bike up Central.

Four dollars for some mutton.

Mamie said Tommy had been asked to run for Parliament.

    I said for the wrong party.

Lived at Waitahuna.

You won't be going anywhere with that hernia.

Out back of the bar on Sunday.

He opened up and the policeman said have you got company?

Put his boot in the door before he could close it.

The Little Sisters.

Delivery with the tanker.

9785243. Two bob each way.

Shut the bloody door!

Used to wear them mucking out the cow byre.

Christ. Now they wear them up the street.

I'm not paying that.

I had a dance with her

and she said don't you remember me?

Up there at Ponderosa. Shangri La.

He pulled me over.

Where are you going at this time of night?
I said I've been at my girlfriend's,
and he laughed,
David, Dick,
the railways isn't a bad sort of job I suppose.

PART TWO

PHONING IT IN

[A response to a cartoon, published in the Otago Daily Times *in December 2019, which used the Samoan measles epidemic as the basis of a joke]*

I'm phoning this one in from the Deep South,
last stop before the road runs out,
the land where time stood still, ran backwards,
dripping a slimy thick shake of shame.

I'm phoning this one in from Dunners, Dun Vegas,
Dudsville, where dunderheads hit bum notes
and sing from the same sheet of dunny paper
in fifty shades of Persil automatic whiteness.

I'm phoning this one in via Jurassic Park
where carbuncled has-beens clap themselves on the back
for their stand against Political Correctness
and snowflakes who are looking to be offended.

I'm phoning this one in for the sniggerers,
the gigglers, the harden-up-get-over-itters,
while lifeless children are lowered into graves
before their parents' disbelieving eyes.

I'm phoning this one in from Pig Island,
South Polynesia, downtown Ōtepoti, Dunedin 9054,
where someone forgot to send the memo
that the natives have feelings too.

I'm phoning this one in from the edge of the map,
the eternal Pacific blue that embraces us,
and joins us together, sea people, island people,
so one day we may see into each other's hearts.

O Sāmoa, from this small place,
for your pain and grief and sorrow
we send our love and ask for forgiveness.
Fa`amālūlū atu

THE HIERARCHY

Invisible homeless
The dead
Care worker
Solo mother (bad suburb)
Loan shark
Bottom feeder
Dolt
Poet
Casual employee
PhD in Fine Arts
Intern
Experimental rodent
Minion
Serf
Serf (creative industries)
Mid-career journalist
Ten years to go and holding on desperately
'Between jobs'
Climate scientist
Aspirational 30-something National voter
Embittered bureaucrat
Accounts
Petty Officer
Solo mother (good suburb)
Will never afford a house but still think they have a chance
Dull but stable
Chief Executive of twelve people

Tobacco lobbyist

Bishop (Destiny Church)

Interior designer

'P' dealer

Change management consultant

Grand Poobah

Dairy farmer, backbone of the nation

'Entrepreneur'

All Black

Admiral of the Whole Damn Fleet

God

Been on *Married at First Sight*

Veitchy

Ex Merrill Lynch currency manipulators

HOW GOOD IS THIS?

After I got back from Honolulu, there were fireworks
for New Year, then cricket, not that I'm complaining,
it's always a busy time of year—a family time.
I was having a look at the business pages one evening
when the wife said look outside at that will ya?
To be honest I couldn't see anything much.
The horizon was a lovely pink colour, or perhaps maroon
or red. The sun was a ball of fire sinking into it.
How good is that? I said to her. But she was
on the iPad, frowning. *Uh-oh* I thought.
I went into the next room and turned up the air con.
I can read a room! Sure enough she followed me through
and said what about this fire then? Haven't heard anything
I said, looking at my phone—of course it was flat.
Then her iPad rang. It was Gladys on Skype.
Where the bloody hell are ya? I heard her crackle.
We've all got to get out of town! I've just got back! I shouted,
people will start complaining if I head off again.
But Gladys told me to look out the window and sure enough
there were these big flames coming over the back fence.
Fuck, said the wife, the joint is going up!
I didn't say anything but I really can't bear it
when a woman uses language like that. I'm old fashioned
at heart. But she was off like the clappers so I went down
after her, and the security bloke who sits at the gate
was waiting for us in the SUV, in fact he was already
off down the drive but the wife waved him down

(the poor bugger nearly ran her over.)
I got in the front and gave him a wink
and said brakes a bit sticky on her mate?
You've got to use a bit of humour to break the ice.
So we were all in snug and I was fiddling around
with the door when this little compartment opened
and a can of lemonade popped out. Cold as.
I said how good is this! but the wife was still on the iPad.
There was this smell, it was pretty disgusting actually,
and I said to the driver someone's burned the prawns
but he said nothing, just turned on the lights and sped up.
I knew then he was a quiet Australian—one of my people.
Anyway we ended up down at Bondi. How good is that?
Everyone was down there. Gladys was waving a torch
and came up with a couple of special branch on either side.
Afternoon boys! I said. For God's sake what are you doing here
she hissed at me. I don't like the Lord's name taken in vain
but she was upset and I didn't take it personally.
I could see a few of the punters pointing to me,
they were waving and yelling G'day I think.
But I couldn't see much with all the smoke.
They must have put on more fireworks because
there were all these bangs—very loud actually,
some of the ladies screamed a bit—then a big cloud
of burning stuff went flying overhead.
I thought it might be a good time to call it a night
but that bloody driver had gone off.
It all got a bit confused after that. We ended up going
for a bit of a paddle and more people started arriving.
I said is that Kylie Minogue over there?

But the wife was in a lather and had started crying
so I tried to give her a cuddle to cheer her up,
but she was being difficult about it to be honest,
so I had to really try hard to get my arms around her
to give her a big squeeze. Women can be a bit like that.
God, get us out of here, I thought to myself.
Then just like that the waters opened.
I mean the ocean went out like the plug had been pulled
and I thought someone up there likes you, fella.
I yelled out come on everyone, follow me!
We walked over the sand and the rock and the mud
where the sea had been, and to be honest
it wasn't that pleasant since there were plastic bags
and an oil platform lying on its side and all the dead fish,
although not as many as you might think.
At one point these kangaroos went racing past.
But the flames kept following us, it was like
the fire knew where we were going. Then all the
grey dead coral sitting on the mud went up like kindling
and it was quite hot so I started running
and when I stopped I was on my own. What to do?
I'm a simple man of faith. So I stood there
and raised my hands to the burning clouds far above
and beseeched O Lord give your humble servant a hand
in his hour of need. Sure enough when I opened my eyes
this big crack in the ground had appeared before me.
I thought to myself, twice in one day! How good is this?
I clambered down into the black crevice
and it was warm and quiet so I kept on
and felt my way and finally came around a corner

and there spreading out in front of me
was an endless plain of fire.

It was the whole world burning.

I turned around because it would have been good
to talk to someone else or get a hug, or just even
shake someone's hand, but there was no one there:
just the darkness and the fire.

THE NATIONAL CONVERSATION

Incurious diodes illuminate the profit centres of Lactopia,
autodidact androids cut hot currency hedges on a midsummer day.

Woke technopreneurs monetise ethnic purity as a niche mode,
tropicana theme bobotels offer three-for-one polar plunge deals

in a hyperborean happy hour in the Arctic of Capricorn.
Post-abundance ice-cube makers replicated from 4D printers

refill Greenland's glacial sheet with frozen dairy megablocks,
streamed by crowd-sourced rubberneckers wielding giant phablets.

Dilated pupils flicker over paywalled premium content,
bamboozled by incompatible delivery platforms.

In the terminal zone of the post-Fordist nine-volume endnote to
    history,
secure protocols are deconstructed by white-hat wizards.

Hop on a moving dot up the exponential curve,
tracking along the towering shadow of Moore's Law.

A client in a giant rabbit onesie in aisle seven
is a semiotic artefact contemplating the heat death of the universe.

In the waiting room of the Dark Enlightenment,
uploaded libertarians automate the expropriated.

Give us this day the milk solids forecast.
Give us this day the hoochy coochy footsie tango

of the Reserve Bank governor semaphoring in Jivvanese
as the Greater Skylandia conurbation goes critical

in a real-time South Sea bubble of ghost suburbs
suspended in the heavenly fragrance of sub-oceanic gas hydrates.

The flower of youth get ubermunted,
highly compressed and resampled in a neoliberal beatbox,

strangers in a strange land, a toxified noosphere
of micromarketing and social media quantum entanglement.

In *Bachelor EnZed*, a cashed-up sociopath jumps the shark,
feels the burn from swivel-eyed chickie babes

and pre-judged by a live stream of scripted reacts
from the data slums of provincial Gigatowns.

The hive mind of the precariat is munching a Pixie Caramel
halfway up the property ladder to the celestial kingdom

in Dirty Dog wraparounds, toting prepaid unlimited texts,
one week away from the event horizon of financial singularity.

The leadership contest is a virtual reality vox pop
from an all-night pyjama party hosted by delirious scream bots.

Great aunts with nothing to hide except pikelet recipes
demand round-the-clock surveillance to confirm their innocence.

A management intern commits to a forty-year famine
to microfinance a deposit on a Westie doer-upper

and eats himself feet first to prove flexibility is the key
to get your foot in the door in a tanking futures market.

The proles are old hat, togged out in elastic-waist pants,
trading in union cards for a Saturday night Megaball ticket.

Pro splicers unzip base pairs on cheap genes,
punt on cows with cubic udders via Trade Me.

From Lenin's tomb to Rob's Mob, the Cold War is deprecated code
as the Warehouse imports Viet Cong singlets by the bin load.

In the deserted hills of Men Alone, the magpies still cry
quardle oodle ardle wardle doodle from cellphone towers.

A five-lane racetrack is drilled out from the underside
of Mount Aspiring's Mr Whippy cone.

Identity politics end in a spaghetti junction of strange loops
where the intersectionally valid stampede symbol manipulators

into a logic gate concealed in an asymmetrical hierarchy
of call outs, call backs and home deliveries.

A waterspout off Punakaiki is a sign of the times,
while a neon taniwha emerges blinking from under

a Road to Nowhere of Significance.
The flag debate is splattered liberally with native batshit

and the National Conversation is a long shriek
filtered through a quadraphonic white-noise generator.

Even in the jaws of this disconsolate season,
the shade of our better selves conjures a memory

of driving through the afternoon in a bubble of now
with the closeness of the loved around us,

past fruit stalls in thunderstorms on the inland straight,
the bitumen to the hills smoky as an evening bay,

our presence suspended in time's shimmer,
dispersed over the GPS co-ordinates of the human heart.

ALTERNATIVE BOOK TITLES FOR AN IMAGINARY AIRPORT BOOKSTORE

How to Read Your Future Doom in Cloud Tops

Curdle It: Culinary delights of the Sahel goat keepers

99 Ways to Expand Your Intestines

Mike Irwin: A life of ineffable normality

Pond Scum at Heart: How our biological origins as primitive algae get in the way of loving relationships

The Void

Climb: Use pointless bureaucratic junkets to secure your place in the economic food chain

Rich Wankers Posing on Third-World Mountainsides

Depression: How it defeated me

Light'n'Peppy

Light'n'Peppy 2, 3 and 4

Mike Irwin: The ordinary years

You Must Be Joking: Ecological tips for frequent flyers about to release another tonne of carbon dioxide into the atmosphere

Failure

Mild Disapproval: The modern liberal's guide to polite concern

An Illustrated Compendium of Celebrity Urinals

Great Plane Disasters

The Internet: My late-night search for the meaning of life with Google

Authentic Insincerity

The Screaming Toddler: The shocking truth of how your parenting skills and inadequate birthday presents are ruining the next generation

Stranger on the Shore: The annotated lyrics of Acker Bilk

Mike Irwin: The next long decade
Dull Walls Colouring Book for Adults
Tits
My Stinking Great Pile of Loot: Life lessons from a toad-like CEO
Home Crafts for the Next Bubonic Pandemic
How to Scrape Toast
Three Jobs and a Pot of Instant Noodles: Magic methods to save a home deposit in 20 years!
The Inner Potato
Colonic Irrigation for Dummies
New Zealand's Top Dishwashing Anecdotes
Bare My Soul: The three-word love poems of Baletcka Moparovia
My Lone Battle Against Daylight Saving
Paperclip Ninja
Oinked: Love and life on an industrial pig farm
Transgender Marsupials of History
Watching Paint Dry: The wisdom of Mike Irwin
Technobutt: The astonishing future of AI toilets

THE PRINCE OF DARKNESS ATTENDS A WORK AND INCOME INTERVIEW

Welcome, Mr Lucifer. Come up. Mind the carpet, please.
I'm sorry the security guard had to ask you to step outside,
but smoking is forbidden on the premises, and brimstone is proscribed
under Health and Safety legislation. I see you have not yet supplied
a clean resumé, or indeed any evidence of actively seeking work.
A pile of ashes won't make the cut. I don't make the rules—
and it would make things simpler if you prepared your resources
prior to our meetings. You may have led a war in heaven,
but in the current market, employers are looking for soft skills.
I note a lack of IT literacy, and the failure to provide references
from a previous employer is troubling: gaps in the CV.
Being cast into outer darkness is a common claim these days.
Slumping in your chair is not advised:
any positions in despair are taken by the Noonday Demon.
With the new incentive process, we have flexibility
to reduce an individual jobseeker's allowance by 50%.
Sloth is no longer acceptable under new directives.
It may be a revelation to you, Mr Lucifer,
but times have changed. I recommend retraining.
There are always openings for those prepared to upskill.
HR and marketing are growth areas which may appeal.
With your experience in middle management, and a renewed focus,
the future may be brighter than you may think.
We look forward to some good news, and if you could,
please mind the carpet on the way back down.

PREMIUM

Insure for future hardship in an uncaring impersonal universe.
Protect your family from stray hairballs and unexpected suds.
Reinforce peace of mind with complimentary beta blockers.
Cushion the impact of the Mauritanian Dengue Pandemic.
Bounce back with an Acts of God supplementary package.
Safeguard your gut wellbeing from attack by rogue flora.
Ameliorate the fallout from cosmic rays in one ezy call.
Cover yourself in event of social media feeding frenzy.
Compensate yourself handsomely for disappointment.
Preserve dignity when others go without toilet tissue.
Secure a front seat in the SpaceX planetary life raft.
Upgrade this policy to win the chance of a lifetime.
Inoculate your assets from creeping stagflation.
Guarantee a cosy respite from life's travails.
Indemnify against The Big One.
Wriggle out of the mess.
Pony up and shell out.
Hedge your bets.
Underwrite.
Atone.

LAND OF THE LONG WHITE ENCRYPTED CLOUD

Flat-lining on the level playing field, buzzed on dairy futures,
the rock-star economy is comatose backstage.
A majestic thunder of white plastic soles echo
along cruise liner gangways, as herds of bucket-listers
clamber up the side of the fish of Māui.
The last orange roughy is blast-frozen, nano-filleted
and punched out through the gravity well
to an orbiting space restaurant called Revolutionary Wealth.
Unfriended by the government, we ask Siri for directions
to a promised land of smart green solutions
and win-win synergies for eco-entrepreneurs.
Our passion is benny bashing, step changes,
wielding killer apps in a financial ecosystem,
humming along to the ready-to-roll Official Cash Rate.
Five Eyes glare on stalks from the cabbage trees
of our Panopticon.
Invisible hunger gnaws the dormitory suburbs
of a Protein Republic.
The Central Committee streams a live feed
from the rumpus room of the dot com mega mansion,
going out in a razzle dazzle of fruit loop tweet bombs
denouncing Islamophobia in Eketahuna,
before uploading to a secure folder
in the land of the long white encrypted cloud.
Imploding press secretaries wrestle the camcorder
from the sweaty palms of bottom-feeding bloggers,
go-to guys for an algorithm of despair.

Mad skillz for the demon operators,
a nation of ten trillion selfies,
fretful sleepers on the doom train of our collective memory,
a half-forgotten melody drowning in a field of binary noise,
dragged under by a swarm of hashtags
on the dark waters of an unknown future.

MAN SOLO

Chain male
poppy smasher
Bali geezer
doer-upper
fridgey freezer
flat screener
dodgy subbie
barbie matey
Tinder swiper
up status typer
Dude Bro
sweet as
drinkey drivey
spacey crazee
chickie baby
hit wit de ladeez
New Year chopout
jandal festy
Xbox gameys
kinda hazey
kinda reggae
kinda thrashy
tinny housey
methy scarey
rum'n'cokey
shit moustachey
work for cashy

cellphone flashy
benny bashy
creepy crawly
roady ragey
clicky porny
webby trolly
FM joker
social smoker
finger poker
sporty barsy
blingey tattie
pimpy ridesey
bigger upper
shouter outer
kick the tyresie
do the dirty
on ya normy
belt buckle
crack a knuckle
leery beersies
cheap and cheeries
crunch the absies
walk the staffies
crack the phatties
rockin Trade Me
shits'n'giggles
change the oilsy
feral dero
good bastardo
meat pie gravy

at the BP
budgie smuggler
small town struggler
do the math bro
travelling lite show
child supporty
titty rater
crush the cansie
late nite bantsie
talk to the handsie
here to party
fridgey freezy
doer-upper
Bali geezer
poppy smasher
chain male

RAGE VIRUS

22 percent of respondents across 142 countries polled by Gallup globally
said they felt angry, which was two percentage points higher than in 2017
and set a new record since the first such survey was conducted in 2006
[*The Washington Post*]

Shirt-fronters face off, munters thump and run,
can't remember landing the king hit.
Craptastic jocks troll the small hours,
spew bile, pour acid, crack the shits.
Red mist filling broken Google Glasses,
living the thug life, living knife crime strife.
Wound tighter than rubber bands,
commuters go ape in five-way snarl-ups.
Triggered vigilantes snap under stress,
ex-employees plot zero-sum vengeance,
flame wars smoulder in icy bedrooms.
Angst in their pants sick dicks throw dick fits
over contested pre-nups in courtroom dramas,
sour pusses get their tits in a tangle,
suck the lemon, get hissy, spit tacks
at the salty, the hangry, the permanently butt hurt.
Teen gamers rage quit Zombie Wars,
reality TV marriages hit the rocks,
love nests reimagined as hate fests.
Killer robots, blue meanies, lone shooters,
face biters getting their mongrel on,
craycray, in a tizzy, pushed over the edge,

mad as cut snakes drinking the hate shake.
He resents her hostile intentions,
she takes offence at his aggressive passivity.
Splenetic, choleric, cold and nasty,
this is how the world ends—
not with a bang, but in a huff.

The climate has always been changing
Greta Thunberg is mentally ill
Dinosaurs didn't drive cars
Greta Thunberg is flying back on a plane
The world was ending fifty years ago
Greta Thunberg should be in school studying
It's a plot by the United Nations
Greta Thunberg could be having fun like a normal teenager
They all go to McDonald's on the way home
Greta Thunberg's extremist parents are to blame
Protesting achieves nothing
Greta Thunberg's yacht sails are made of oil
Teenagers think they know everything
Greta Thunberg is a globalist puppet
No one would go if it was the school holidays
Greta Thunberg is paid by George Soros
It snowed last week
Greta Thunberg is alienating moderates
It is part of God's plan
Greta Thunberg is a false flag op by the Deep State
Socialism doesn't work
Greta Thunberg is an over-privileged brat
Plants love carbon
Greta Thunberg is an enemy of freedom
So-called scientists are on the gravy train
Greta Thunberg is needlessly worrying young people
In the long run we're all dead anyway
and they all have mobile phones

INTERPRETATIONS TOWARDS A CONTEMPORARY THEOLOGY

There was darkness without end.
The shape sat heavy on a floor of mud.
It fondled a nameless urge.
The shape said let there be light.
Let there be some fucken light in here.
A fluoro tube buzzed into existence.
The shape looked upon the mud.
It thought, I could fuck some shit up.
For six days and nights,
it moulded mud with care
into a great rough sphere.
On the seventh day
it left this pustule for a rest.
It chilled with a six pack
until some half-life stirred
on the surface of its globe.
From the wobbly jelly
a man stepped forward;
the heavens wept with shame.
From a trunk of bones
the shape pulled a crooked stick,
created woman, and moved on her,
just like a bitch.
In both their breasts
the shape set a beating doom
which made them stagger

incomplete, from room to room,

driven by their endless need,

each carrying half a seed.

And the shape said:

Let there be *guns*, let there be *pizza*, let there be *motorways*, let there be *casinos*, let there be *shock jocks*, let there be *brands*, let there be *pussy grabbing*, let there be *flying machines raining death from the sky*, let there be *children who work upon the landfills*, let there be *McFlurrys*, let there be *great towers above the desert*, let there be *oil and fire and burning waters*, let there be *weeping*, let there be *smiting of the queers and the freaks*, let there be *bent cops*, let there be *complex financial products*, let there be *albums of instrumental Christmas songs in reggae style*, let there be *jeans*, let there be *resorts*, let there be *the broken sleeping in the streets*, let there be *dog shit everywhere*, let there be *loyalty cards*, let there be *cryptocurrencies*, let there be *idolaters and Pharisees and sorcerers*, let there be *nerve gas*, let there be *just enough hope*, let there be *fucking*, let there be *energy drinks*, let there be *a multitude of exotic cancers*, let there be *the pursuit of happiness*.

And there was; and the shape looked upon the dead oceans, and saw that it was good.

THE GIRLS WENT OFF

and when they came back they had become women
while we had filled hours and months with our works.
It seems a short day since they walked past,
hair draped on the sleeve of an oversized leather jacket,
haughty, vulnerable, half-amused, fluent in their charm.
We awoke in restless dark to their new unfamiliarity.
They had scars and history. They had crossed wide lands.
A river of blood and brine ran as they silently stood.
From this torrent came terrible and wonderful things.
The insurrection of life in the glow of a 3am hospital.
A doctor lifting a child from a crimson slice. *Baby is out.*
A gasp before the wail of life, a singularity
of dense energy greedily sucking atmosphere.
This was just one of many possible dreams.
In unnoticed years, some ascended conduits of power.
Some remained among the living, in corridors of obscure toil.
Others waited out the grief of winter.
What blinds them to our nature that they try again and again?
We struggle to translate their scrawled notes, their utterances,
the remote hurt flickering in their clouded eyes.

THE 21st-CENTURY BOOK OF DOOM

Indexed by Dow Jones, Table of Contents courtesy of End Times
Incarcerated, the *Book of Doom* is a must-read chart topper eye
popper for the New Jaded.
Couriered by drone to the compromised privacy of your home,
interior decorating for the mental architecture of your chrome dome.
In Dante's *Inferno*, new circles are devised by crowdsourced ghost
hackerz, send them on down, the finance sector mad hatters
drinking dry the top shelf antimatter.
Hitting the panic buttons, sitting in our panic rooms:
We are all writing in the Book of Doom.

Instant humans get their kicks, just add water to the mix,
read between the lines to the rhythm of doomsday clock ticks.
Reserve banksters roll the presses, print money they can't buy,
all typeset by a million philosopher monkeys, channelling dead
white guys.
Time-poor wage slaves pay to play canned exotica in shades of grey,
while the eternal teleprompter of the soul tells us just what to say.
Hitting the panic buttons, sitting in our panic rooms:
We are all writing in the Book of Doom.

First World hysterichondriacs going viral in camouflage hazmat
suits, political party animals with their mitts on the loot shrieking
rooty toot toot.
A barcoded beast lays on the irony in a Revelations roadshow,
handing out mini pizzas promoting 0800 WARM GLOW.
Checking the inbox for fond postcards from a sentient spambot,

Asset-stripping front-bench lovelies in a national fire sale of the whole
damn lot.
Hitting the panic buttons, sitting in our panic rooms:
We are all writing in the Book of Doom.

THE CONTAGION

Despite Google and experts, it's fair to say
it caught us off guard—by surprise.
There was not a lot of *joined up thinking,*
and early on in the piece, some wondered
how such an antique doom could still
stalk the land with scythe and skull.
Towns slammed their gates,
the plague already inside the walls.
Measures were taken, and when those
measures did not suffice, other methods
were reclaimed from shadowed past.
The aged and weak abandoned
in long moaning corridors,
breath crushed out by winged goblins
crouched on their chests.
Our isolated selves gathered by screens
and we followed by tweet, post, insta,
the leisurely progress of an end.
Kings must once have gaped
at flames eating the mounds of dead
in town squares. Our leaders,
versed in modern politics,
negotiated with the contagion.
They spoke of stimulus, negative growth
for consecutive quarters,
soothing us in our troubled sleep.

DISCARD ARCHIPELAGO

Across the earth it rolls, in unfathomable cubits,
titanic and prodigious, from horizon to horizon,
from sump to quagmire, necrotic outgrowth of the technium,
obituary to Protean craft, voltage spent.
Luminous pools simmer under the anoxic monsoon,
acid corrodes lake's rim, flowers of fire bloom,
torpid vapours smoulder night long into half-lit day,
tangled cables spilling from a Gorgon's skull.
Over the diabolic maps of motherboards,
gusts rattle alphabets of teeth, and on the seas,
armadas of dull plastic form a discard archipelago
spanning the sightless eyes of dead screens.

THE WORLD ENDS

The world ends with a handcrafted thick shake from Domino's
The world ends with a black sea closing above you
The world ends with a Sarah Huckabee Sanders press conference
The world ends with big emotions from a slam poet
The world ends with a swarm of antibiotic-resistant microbes
The world ends with Astrud Gilberto singing 'Corcovado'
The world ends with Alpha Females on the board of directors
The world ends with a squinty-eyed TV pundit getting it wrong
The world ends with a child support payment letter
The world ends with flame and ice
The world ends with the King of Broken Hearts
The world ends with the ultimate wipe-out on *Surfin' Safari*
The world ends with a quiet shutting of the door
The world ends with a billionaire's country club on Mars
The world ends with the Pope whipping out a giant doobie
The world ends with a skinny polar bear floating face down
The world ends with a lost password to Netflix
The world ends with you out at the dairy buying a toilet roll
with a Kenny G sax solo drifting on the evening air
with the lawns unmown, the bills unpaid
The world ends with ten years in an inexpensive rest home
and killer bees in the air conditioning
The world ends with the internet breaking up with us
The world ends with foodies gobbling braised organic rhino turd
The world ends with an Emin7 chord
The world ends with a convergence of mutually reinforcing
    convergences

The world ends with the sun swelling like a giant melon
The world ends with endless pornography but no babies
The world ends with the upload of consciousness to the fifth
    dimension
The world ends with a killer asteroid the size of Oklahoma
The world ends with a kid saying *I'm bored*

PART THREE

ESPLANADE, 1979

In the pelagic demisphere of Zealandia,
longitudinal waveforms make landfall,

saline reference points to a boy's dream,
a salt song on the border of night's shore.

East of the lone streetlamp,
my hungry eyes parse inscriptions

of kelp cable, bleached shells, plastic cords
cast aside from the merchant ships

that wait before the harbour's neck.
Sea mulch, sea fluff, sea clutter,

posted through the gyre and whorl
of swell maps and submarine rivers.

In the sea of lost time I navigate
from reef to port to coast of memory,

mark a line down a mile of sand
with a crooked stick, I wade summer-deep

in shallows, body-surf a flummox of foam,
balls frozen, brine chafing at my skin.

On shore, my father (in blue trunks)
wields a sun-bent tennis racquet.

From the dim veranda I catch sight
of the nacreous sheen of porpoises,

barreling down tubes of green glass.
Behind the beige and taupe of the long spit,

crabs teeter on the estuary floor,
bubbles pop, exhaled from cool silt.

Black swans, delicate glyphs, mark the lagoon.
On this temperate coast,

with its garbled topographies of broken clay,
marble-eyed fish, delinquent gulls,

I sift sea pools for ambient life,
then I am already walking homeward

to find the future that awaits formless.
Dank fog coils over the headland

before winter turns into blunt heat
buzzing off the land, drifts forever

rearranging the neck of the coast,
patterned dunes replying to the waves,

capped by sprays of spiky marram,
and the crackle of lupin pods springing seeds across the air.

LIVING IN THE MANIOTOTO

Driving west on a long weekend,
our car follows the undulating pass
between hulking peaks devoid of human trace,
then the long inland straight across the flats.
Out to the south, a sluggish river winds
young and slender, and fences angle across
hard-scrabble acres of grey lucerne.
At gravel's end, a sign swings on knotted wire:
    Cosy Dell.
Trev stubs a smouldering rollie on a fence post.
Val busy at the bench. Lunch served on Formica.
In the lounge, the party line warbles a mystery code.
They only get one television channel here,
to blether Sunday repeats and conceal
the dome of sky, the maddening winds.
A final generation of small-holders, part-timers,
seeing out the years with the county council,
the timber yard, the post office counter.
Dogs in their kennels whine. Pigs grunt
affably out back. The shed's piled roof-high
with eccentric tools, jars of odd screws,
hanging chains, electric spools.
The children, grown, have left this place for good.
The bungalow, red-brick, iron-roofed
stands alone on the encircling, unknowable plain.
We wave and wave from our windows,
as their figures standing by the gate
recede into our dream-memory.

SELENE

'Her great orbit is full, and then her beams shine brightest as she
    increases.
So she is a sure token and a sign to mortal men.'

['To Selene', *The Homeric Hymns*]

On the silken mud of the estuary floor
the sea is drawn from the channel's branch,
creeping semi-diurnal under her spell
in this ragged rainy corner of the planet,
stranded amongst white sand and clouds.
Lying in bed, window ajar,
I listened to the dialect of waves long ago
and perhaps in late evening's cool,
I saw the sprinkled motes of our galaxy
circle in infinitude above, a dust of faint luminance.

THE SPIT

Kua kite te kōhanga kuaka? Who has seen the nest of the kuaka?

[Māori proverb]

Gradients. From lead to ash to bone white.
From shore to shallow to deep. Dividing the bulge of the Pacific
and relentless, endless sky, flows an omniscience,
a prayer, a pantheon of godwits, aloft on grand tour.
Emerging from boreal desolation, from crepuscular light,
piercing tropic-salted mist to landfall on fine sands,
in the heat shimmer of the south.
As a child I wandered the frilled hem of sea
and studied their huddled circles on a windward coast,
these slight modest creatures, who with controlled drift
span magnetic latitudes, at home in the world.

A LIFT

Memory grows slight and tangled.
I handle it with care,
account for its balance,
its shapes of recollection.
A white shirt hung,
neck grey from two days' wear.
Crumbs, windows slick,
steaming tea, the heater's orange tubes.
Winter on inland hills,
drifting cloud and cloud above,
as our Ford Escort chuckles along
streets oil-black with drizzle.
At the school gates,
I join the idle and reluctant,
with no intent.
Factory sirens summon.
My father drives away
wrapped close against the day,
through leafless trees
to the city, dawn-pale, drawn.

QUANTUM DECOHERENCE AT A BAILTER SPACE GIG, 1989

20 July was my seventeenth birthday
and I went to Sammy's on a Thursday night.
Cold and rain, a winter standard for Dunedin.
My one clear memory is standing alone
on a fairly empty dance floor,
spotlit by a stream of sodium-blue light
while feeling my neural networks
being reformatted by a subsonic phase shift
on top of which an avalanche of white noise
glued loosely together with a standing wave
of human-friendly harmonic frequencies
pulsed from side to side of the hall
while bodies swayed like reeds in a gale.
When I left some time after midnight
life had changed permanently,
and my inner ears were filled
with a softly anaesthetic snowfall.

CITY OF BASTARDS

There was a commotion outside the window.
Millions arrived in the night and built
petrol stations, delicatessens and strip joints.
Signs point everywhere you cannot go.
I think of the past to hold myself down.
There are more products than you can imagine,
throttled streets lined with plates of black ice.
I sift endless papers that rustle with a faded sound.
Nicotine eyes stare without relief.
Houses are pulverised by hornet-painted demons.
There have been twenty darknesses of terror
and black shapes twirling fire in the avenues,
banging on walls, screaming cats and violent pauses
between days and nights and days.
Everyone wears the same inscrutable mask.
The rain conceals us when we drive onwards
down the tributaries of the Underworld.

SO AS NOT TO WAKE

There was the before. There was the present.
Afterwards there is another city.
Walking at night the stars float beyond the hills.
To fragile senses the council flats are almost beautiful.
The cubes of light suspended high above.
After unaffordable drinks and phoney blather,
inhaling cool wet air with relief.
Certain moments are anxious with forgetting.
Teeth bite hard on the insides.
Ghost imprints of faded routines spark and fizzle,
radio signals from lost civilisations.
Watching a movie, a tear slips down in the scene
when the cartoon mammoth dies. That's how it is now.
Concrete steps and an old carpet thinned by years.
Belong for now where the corridor is a dark eternal mouth.
Go in and out. Keep a tidy desk. Order is important.
Think back over days in multitude, in blurred echelon,
and wonder who was there, what was said.
Outside, the wave of night rolls on.
Within, an acid pool simmers. A grown-up will survive.
The tangle of nerves and strings cannot be teased free.
Go at them with scissors: tear out long roots.
Clutching in every corner of life, in the way the door
is closed gently when returning late at night,
so as not to wake,
so as not to wake.

ALGEBRA

More questions. Distance = electricity x our voices.
The tree is running September through its arms
and a fountain eats away at a stone bowl.
There are several possible solutions.
Cold life of waves falling on the shore.
Magnesium flame melting in the night.
Forty days built from clay and sun and blood.
A room that seems larger on the inside.
The thirst of a walker in the hills.
In a cemetery in the afternoon, small birds
calling from one gravestone to the next.
A blue vase of unknown origin,
a cliff descending to the ocean,
an envelope with a lock of hair,
our voices meeting and holding one another,
delicate hooks suspended in the atmosphere.

EDGE OF SHADOW

Blank light envelops an empty hour
of being stranded in time and place,
amongst what has gone and what awaits.
Silent sky sun-struck, clover parasols tremble
and honey bees hover on balmy updrafts,
dancing on daisy cones and paper petals.
Suspended in the quantum uncertainty of now,
humid notes rise from entangled grass,
lambent apples swell with green hardness.
Boughs ripple in metallic susurration,
slow explosions distilled in summer's end.
Eternal clouds dissemble and ubiquitous Wi-Fi
streams code packets across the afternoon.
Rusted leaves spell the retreat of life.
Evening drains away earlier each night.
Trade winds stolen south circulate,
a cat scuttles, lamp eyes staring.
In the kitchen's shadow, an electric jug crackles.
Orange lamps string the hills,
and we could be anywhere.

CENTRAL REDUX

Shadows flicker beneath greenstone waters
where the past is inundated by a billion litres,
and a spectral road fathoms deep
leads through the drowned valley of an inland sea.

Megafauna of state capitalist uberdevelopment
plug the valley's neck below constellations of tussocks,
dusky anemones on a reef of ironclad ranges
and gravel berms beside ice-blue streams.

Honest stonefruit and dust-stained ewes are crowded out
by vigorous hybrids of economic gene splicing:
boutique wineries self-seeded from the grey soil,
fat grapes liberally irrigated by cashflow liquidity

while first-world psychodramas play out
in skyscapes of high-altitude heli-tourism
as paragliding dice rollers snap selfies
from mid-point vortices in death plunges.

Once a destination for steam-power diasporas,
Hibernian chancers and Cantonese exiles
are suspended in a hologram of alluvial gold flecks
and Victorian era get rich quick schemes.

Snowflakes spindrifting in a timeshare wonderland,
where scratchings and etchings on the hills

annotate a century of busywork by scrappy toilers,
their faded palimpsest of efforts now redundant.

A five-mile-tall nimbus blobs out on the horizon,
contemplating the innovation of stone-baked pizzerias.
Zigzag peaks recede behind scenic double glazing,
freeze frames in the tuck and knead of the tectonic kitchen.

A grid subdividing the heart in an eternal revision
of the district plan, where financial wizards
drop dark currency on rustic homesteads,
intent on eco-satori behind security protocols.

Fine living features in pull-out supplements
feed an arms race of aspirational overcompensation,
made-it matrons wrestling the power steering
in late-model Eurotrash SUVs the size of oxen.

A rubber tube steers away on glacial melt
before jet boat hearties short circuit the bay
with a rude burst of gurgling clangour,
shattering the crystal heat of the afternoon.

Tag teams of blue-arse blowflies,
opportunists loitering on a sad lamb carcass:
pink blossoms hammered flat
by a cold front's frigid grapeshot.

Fire alert on permanent high, Naseby's sluiced clays
are colonised by the lime shimmer of exotic larches,

while an optimistic billboard counsels the weary
Avoid Fatigue—Stop At Ranfurly.

The silence of the Maniototo is a blank totality,
an inverse shockwave of nothing.
Above Ida Valley, wild thyme sprinkles slopes
in a purple haze over rubble and bones.

Rows of dinged utes cool off in front of rural pubs,
lonely as dead-end roads, drinkers whiling the hours
hidden from the infinite heavens and day-long tempests,
awaiting the postponed judgement of the long now.

Above Wakatipu, plastic bubbles ascend in parallel symmetry
to provide a ten-dollar view of million-dollar apartments,
lakeside gloom pooling in the lengthening evening,
as Airbuses touch down in a sweet end-times aroma of peak oil.

PORT CHALMERS

Port, Dogtown, Kōpūtai, names good and ill,
you look outward to oceans, waiting for the world.
Cruise liners and log boats snuggle wharves.
A thousand trunks of *Pinus radiata* are matchsticks
piled before a crow's nest lookout,
the channel a blue stripe on ruffled green fur.
Ships glide through the throat of the harbour,
models inserted into the glass bottle of summer.
Nudged under the crook of cliffs, a camel's hump
scattered with draughty villas and stone churches,
where wharfies in orange overalls pop in to the café
for a flash coffee, or pie from the dairy.
From ships we live, proclaims the bronze plaque:
and now in place of wool and frozen carcass
are megacubits of golden butter,
the determined tramp of tracksuited pensioners
embarking from *Princess of the Seas*.
Steam curls in fluffy ventings from flanks
of looming woodchip mountains,
while the permanent hum of industry pervades,
wasp-yellow diggers growling across yards,
lanky straddles speed-looping the terminal with boxes
to stack and stow in perpendicular precision.
When I was twenty, buzzed on magic mushrooms,
I walked around the fence to Back Beach,
watching giant machines in shadowless glare,
feeling the subterranean drumming

of a goods train clambering through the tunnel.
Now monster trucks change down with a roar
on George Street, where crusty old hands
mix with try-hard metropolitan newbies
wandering the retro boutiques where bohemians
assemble in creative endeavour.
The grey page of evening is inscribed
by the querulous drone of free noise guitar improv,
the demented squawk of a feral rooster,
the clink of bottles from the rugby clubrooms.
Channel lights wink the way home
in a cheery salute of green and red.

FROM THE QUEEN STREET WENDY'S

Hello Auckland, my old friend, a concrete block
topped by scraggly palms in ornamental pots.
Cosmopolitan for sure, but the colour's leached
in your overexposed glamour shot.
In unaccounted time, I walk. It's half familiar.
Twenty years swallowed by the yawp of age.
Now I understand there was nothing to understand.
Outside Father Ted's Irish Bar,
Mammon blows smoke rings into his mobile phone.
Tired hipsters grouch over toy coffees,
sleeves tactically rolled, expressing their inked attitude.
On the street corner a poet appears, baffled.
'It seems so depressing!'—this economic powerhouse
marooned in a hypoxic ocean of capital gains.
In the games room, rows of pokies chortle,
cheery brutes with gullets hungry for coins.
Faces tender with hope before screens
flickering in a warm fug of desperation.
I drift sleepwards inside sea-green glass
beneath the tower's one-fingered salute.
Have I won? (The hush says yes—silence is golden.)
At least survived, but like most, half broken inside.

AUTUMN IN THE SOUTH

The first leaves are fallen and the eye of an itinerant gull
returns to flakes of crust scattered at the feet
of lunchtime diners in the Queens Gardens.
Temporary custodians of the daylight world,
marooned on an island encircled
by the bitumen rivers of the one-way system.
Intimations of mortality under the shadowline
of the cenotaph, marble unwarmed
and blank as oblivion to the late sun of March.
Victoria turns her back and glares.
The young step past in remote mediascapes
streaming through bonewhite pods and earbuds.
On the way down to winter's fathoms
in the counter-clockwise reverse geography
of the southern latitudes, the oceanic dream of the Pacific,
a party of school children scamper and giggle
beneath white slabs and the southern sun tracks
another degree, to the implacable, patient horizon.

CAPRICORN AND BUNKER

Shadows flicker on mottled sand,
a manta's cloak pulses languid beats.
Limbs reach from fractal colonies,
from the gigapolis of intricate sprawl.
Bommies bootstrap in symbiotic increments,
dreaming towers of calcification.
Distant breakers crest the outer wall,
chuntering against sessile armour.
Cephalopods perambulate skeletal encasements,
slip through interstitial crevasses.
These southern reefs are beige and ivory,
manufactured by nano-clones
doomed by the outrages of the Anthropocene.
Red as Christmas, a shell-helmeted crab
scrambles, navigating tracks of egg-heavy turtles.
Heliotropium, Casuarina, Grand Devil's Claws,
branches ripe with heat-doped noddies,
guano stink mingling with sweet ocean wind.
Goggled strangers, we drift the maze of lagoon,
until at last, exhausted by fecundity,
the slop of wavelets and our rasping breath,
we surface and make for shore.
Salt-swollen, skin tight with sun,
returned to humanworld's temporary hum.
An evening breeze slaps at the canvas.
The world lights up, flecked by darting birds.
Fleets of swollen cumulus
trundle in formation over Capricornia.

BAT FLU

At first it's novelty.
A chance to catch up on housework.
Garden trimmers burst into life.
Unwanted noise becomes reassurance,
a signal of normality over the hedge.
But the world's grown strange
beyond the letterbox.
The government prints money,
gives it away. It's early days:
cupboards still half full,
accounts still in the black,
a vicarious global crisis over the horizon
where great cities thresh like wounded whales
and pimp politicians root around
in the muck for a quick fix, an easy blame.
But it's just a matter of time,
before the horizon catches up with us.
An invisible miasma folds itself over the land.
Bat-spawned superbug, cellular neutron bomb,
pirate RNA throwing grappling hooks
over the side of our civilian organisms.
The day the earth stood still, the week,
then month, when things in general just stopped,
went slo mo, ran out of juice.
Streets bereft of clamour.
Some have to get on with it.
Gowned medics, checkout chicks,
remote database admins in midday PJs.

The patient and the tense queue
and avoid looking at each other
in case infection can shimmy down
a casual glance.
Phony war, evolution's arm race,
everything's a means to an end
for these microscopic time travellers
and their nasty ways.
The world is suspended in its own bubble.
Keeping our distance,
we somehow become closer.

THE EARTH FROM SPACE

On perihelion, a glass pupil dilates
and swallows the horizon,
an infinitude of bits arranged
in reflection of the globe below.
The marbled fat of oriental tempests,
striated runes on rusted desert heights.
The Pacific a white line trembling
before the Andean cordillera.
Terraced slopes, polygons of verdant rice,
the snaggled fang of a subcontinent
spangled with pulsing circuitry.
Dairy whip caps the South Pole,
the Andaman Sea a peacock tail,
green eyes flashing in royal blue.
Data feeds ping off comms satellites
in zettabytes of decontextualised space dust.
Our alien sphere rolls on through the airless night.

GREAT SOUTH DESERT

Te Ika-a-Māui and Te Wai Pounamu are amalgamated,
welded fast by the gnarled spine of a metamorphic Taniwha
manifested in the Great Uplifting of 2035.

Shattered cliffs bombard the Kaikōura coast with rubble.
Genetically reimagined moa gently graze amongst
abandoned dairy installations of the Mackenzie badlands.

Goat herds, feral and feckless, wander the Great South Desert.
Typhoons deconstruct malls, peeling roofs like bananas
throughout the Golden Triangle conurbation.

A permanent storm cell hovers from Karamea to Haast,
sluicing depopulated extra-terrestrial terroramas
of munted infrastructure and imploded mineshafts.

Ten-metre hi-voltage fences fortify the opaque globe
of Club Xanadu on Wakatipu's privatised lakefront
where drones emerge from ash clouds delivering pods

of platinum-class refugees to the shimmering pleasure dome.
Waves trace salty fingers on the lip of coast, exposing landfills
of toner cartridges and mummified, post-dated vindaloos.

Dull heat baffles survivors hiding from the killer sun
in their valleys. Above the hypersaline, blood-warm lagoon,
the skeleton of a dead stadium stands sentinel.

THE SPHERE

Once on, there is no way off.
All paths will cross eventually (in theory).
Gravity grasps all to its stony lap.
You often wonder how you got here,
or got anywhere. The answer's never clear.
You walk upon the sphere.
The sphere looks outward,
for its innards are only mineral and hot mud.
There are tasks to be done,
and they are done to varying degrees of success.
Some close to perfection.
Our tasks sprinkle the surface with tiny dancing points.
Our journeys grow longer
but still blink in and out momentarily.
Each day we steal from the sphere,
the weight sucks stronger by the year.
Tasks become ends in and of themselves.
We resign ourselves to circularities,
and walk upon the sphere.

PART FOUR

DARK WATER

There is nothing here for you.
There is no light above the door that says that home is near.
You will not cast your arms around your father's neck
and rest your head in the bedroom's evening quiet.

There is nothing here for you.
There is no laughter nor a mother's lips to calm your tears.
You will not see the summer clouds of the land they sought,
but breathe the smell of fear and diesel fumes upon the night.

There is nothing here for you.
There are no voices from the kitchen talking gently as you sleep.
You will not learn new songs or squabble with your brother now.
Dark water draws the warmth from life.
Dark water fills our hearts.

48° 14.5′ S, 168° 18.76′ E

*[Person overboard, 70 kilometres south of Rakiura/Stewart Island,
New Zealand, 24 January 2004]*

It's not a sea. It's ocean.
Brood black skies and so cold it burns.
Vo Minh Que, twenty-two months of ship time, no kid,
picked up by the whipping line and tossed
like a doll into four-metre swells
from a floating death sentence called the *Tasnui*,
slopping around due south of Rakiura.
They call them factory trawlers.
Too glamorous by half—
shitbuckets splattered with rust,
with a tangled shitbucket heap of wires, gears, mesh.
Vo Minh Que, thirty-three summers deep in life,
remained visible for one to one-and-a-half hours.
They threw three lifebuoys, ten lifejackets, fishing floats,
while he floundered, kicked then slipped away.
Down below, the factory floor knee-deep with carcasses.
They slide around in blood and brine
while men rip fish heads off with buzzing blades.
Vo Minh Que, Vietnamese national,
no home town mentioned, no outrage,
no diplomatic incident reported.
His last link the sweaty office
of a crewing agent far from this sightless deep.
They pack bruised flesh in ice,

sweep the excess into the waves
for a trail of seagulls to scream over.
The report from the maritime office
was tidy and concise.
Vo Minh Que, your memorial is archived data,
and perhaps the tears of a mother.
At about 2000 hours, when the deceased
was no longer visible, the crew heaved in the nets
and informed the shore authorities.
Under Korean flag state regulations,
no records are required to be kept
on treacherous strands of wire.
Vo Minh Que, whose last haul dragged
writhing fins and gasping gills from benthic gloom,
whose hands placed this white flesh on our table,
and whose long days profited someone far away
from this place of endless wind and salt.
It's not a sea. It's ocean.

SNOW COUNTRY

The negations of the place. Raw perimeter is scarred.
Wounds of blown ragged rock punched in the coast.
The diesel stench reminds of cause and effect.
A new refugee ship wends through the chessboard of shards.
Machines bite at the flanks of mountains.
Syringes probe and plunge mineral veins.
Dark flecks hover, drone feeds streaming back to the hungry ghosts.
We work. Ant-like figures in our filthy safety wear.
In grey concrete halls we tend our gardens: plastic vats slimed with
    algae.
We cultivate proteins and throw the slop to locusts.
We are beyond hate. The old cities have long since burned,
the jade powder of their smashed windows mixed with blood.
The passions of grief have settled. There were the first children.
Now we are the last, begat by you.
There is numb fucking and drugs and some run into the darkness.
The worst is the terrible hope that keeps us all through winter,
the murmuring in the close air of the shelters.
The night is old and inhuman. There are reports of war.
You might ask, but where are the young?
Above, the orbital habitats of billionaires flicker silently.

LAND

The coastal plains are denuded of ice, colonised by weeds,
inchoate forests of stunted life. The churned moraine expands.
Glacial tongues slaver. Katabatic winds pour from the interior.
In a grey torrent, boulders tumble like dice.

This primal deluge ploughs through to the rim of the continent,
plumes in arterial bursts against the blue.

SEA

An endless armada of icebergs drifts north,
circling gyres, their pinnacles shadowing waves.
In the glaucous dim of summer night their growls echo.
The perpetual storm of the south collides with Capricornian winds.
Fishing fleets scour but the seas have forgotten the dialects of life.
Nets brush through stillborn silence, until the ships return north,
sweltering in torpid haze, nudging aside a gigamass of plastic.
The equatorial storms are violent, unpredictable, monstrous,
yet the old codes no longer claim allegiance.
A distress call is swallowed up amidst the churning rage,
the vast unwitnessed death of the ocean.

OCEAN OF TENTACLES

A scientific article notes the ongoing global population growth of cephalopods (squid, cuttlefish and octopuses) due to changing environmental conditions in the world's oceans [ABC news, May 2016]

A cyan sea encircles cracked coasts,
empty lands, deserted cities.
Dust and concrete bakes under swollen sun,
but no human heart is left to pity.

Yet in the acid brine, shadows stir,
and with the dance of sand they come.
Yellowed eyes from older times
stare from smooth oval craniums.

Under blanched coral's jagged trees,
they gather in the shallows.
When all else fades and dies away,
they feast in turn upon their fellows

and multiply in their domain,
to feel their way across the shores.
The ocean of tentacles has come alive,
and follows life's blind law.

THE HADAL ZONE

Pressure bends life from its mould.
Night is absolute, eternal, cold.
From the realm of light above
a marine snow falls in drifts
to settle in the sightless deep.
There is survival, but no love where
pressure bends life from its mould.
Night is absolute, eternal, cold.

ENVOI

SONG OF THE SEA

The wind is blowing from the sea,
it scatters salt on childhood dreams.
I lie awake with my torch and read.
The wind is blowing from the sea.

The wind is blowing in the trees,
I walk with a girl of seventeen
through half-lit streets, just her and me.
The wind is blowing in the trees.

The wind is blowing from the hills,
now I sleep and work and swallow pills
and make paper darts from all the bills.
The wind is blowing from the hills.

The wind blows cold upon the shore,
as you think of what came before
and wait upon time's unbending law.
The wind blows cold upon the shore.

The wind is blowing all night long,
and from its thread it sews a song
you once were here, but now you have gone.
The wind is blowing all night long.

ACKNOWLEDGEMENTS

Some of the poems in this collection have previously appeared in *Landfall*, *takahē*, *Newsroom*, *The Spinoff*, *Minarets*, *Meniscus*, *Down in Edin*, *NB* (Dunedin Public Libraries magazine), *Poetry New Zealand Yearbook*, *The Perfect Weight of Blankets at Night* (NZ Poetry Society anthology, 2019), *Cordite*, *The Friday Poem*, *Pantograph Punch*, *Manifesto Aotearoa: 101 political poems* (Otago University Press, 2017), *Brief*, *Mimicry*, the *Otago Daily Times* and the *Phantom Billstickers Cafe Reader*.

Thank you to Steve Braunias, David Eggleton, Sue Wootton, James Norcliffe, Carolyn McCurdie, Duncan Eddy, Caroline Davies, Sarah Jane Barnett, Jack Ross, Erena Shingade, Philip Temple, Emma Neale, Holly Hunter, Deb Wain, Sandra Arnold, Raewyn Alexander, Olivia Macassey, Lisa Gorton, Mez Breeze, Simon Groth and Kent MacCarter for originally publishing some of these poems.

Thanks to all the Otago University Press family: Rachel Scott, Fiona Moffat, Laura Hewson, Imogen Coxhead, Arvin Lazaro and Vanessa Manhire.

My great appreciation to editor Emma Neale and my spiritual adviser, Michael Steven.

My gratitude for friendship and creative inspiration to Bill Martin, Alexandra Bligh, Andrew Spittle, Sally Lonie, John Howell, Rachel Bailey, Mike Irwin, Nicky Page, the University Bookshop (Dunedin), and The Alpha Plan. Love and appreciation to the extended Billot family: Harry and Eunice, Yvette and Duncan, Hector, George, Reg and Ernest, and special thanks to Susie Ripley.

Victor Billot was born in Dunedin in 1972. He has worked in communications, publishing and the maritime industry. In 2020 he was commissioned by the Newsroom website to write a series of political satires in verse. His poems have been displayed in the Reykjavik City Hall and in Antarctica.